# THE DOLLARS AND CENTS WIPE-OFF BOOK

## SCHOLASTIC INC.

New York   Toronto   London   Auckland   Sydney
Mexico City   New Delhi   Hong Kong

D0840728

# HOW TO USE THIS BOOK

1. Study the QUICK DOLLAR & CENT GUIDE pages to see how much each denomination is worth.
2. Note how different coins and dollars put together can add up to the same amount.
3. Beginning with the PENNIES, NICKELS & DIMES page, fold the flap on the back cover over the answers and start adding your money.
4. Write your answers in the boxes on the flap next to each question **with a grease pencil or an erasable felt-tip pen.**
5. Check your answers. How did you do?
6. If all the answers are correct, erase them with a damp cloth and move on to the next page.
7. If you missed any answers, go back and review the QUICK DOLLAR & CENT GUIDE pages and try again.

## GOOD LUCK!

No part of this publication may be reproduced in whole or in part, or stored in a retrieval system, or transmitted in any form or by any means, electronic, mechanical, photocopying, recording or otherwise, without written permission of the publisher. For information regarding permission, write to Scholastic Inc., Attention: Permissions Department, 555 Broadway, New York, NY 10012.

ISBN 0-590-68706-9

Copyright © 1998 by FOUR HARTS, INC.
All rights reserved. Published by Scholastic Inc., 555 Broadway, New York, NY 10012.

SCHOLASTIC and associated logos are trademarks and/or registered trademarks of Scholastic Inc.

12 11 10 9 8 7 6 5 4 3 2 1    8 9/9 0 1 2 3 4/0

Printed in the U.S.A.         23
First Scholastic printing, October 1998

# QUICK CENT GUIDE

1¢ =

5¢ =  =

10¢ =   =

25¢ =   =

50¢ =  =

$1 =  =

# QUICK DOLLAR GUIDE

$1 =

$5 = =

$10 = =

$20 = =

$50 = =

$100 = =

# PENNIES, NICKELS & DIMES

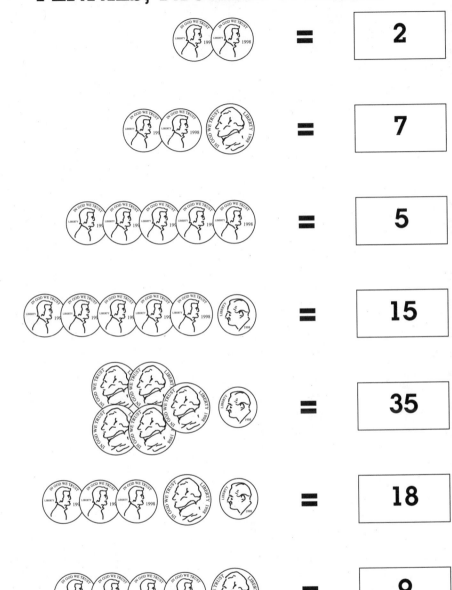

= 2

= 7

= 5

= 15

= 35

= 18

= 9

= 24

# QUARTERS & HALF DOLLARS

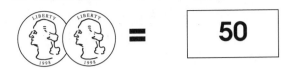 = 50

 = 75

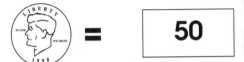 = 50

 = 75

 = 1.00

 = 1.00

 = 1.25

 = 2.00

# ONES, FIVES & TENS

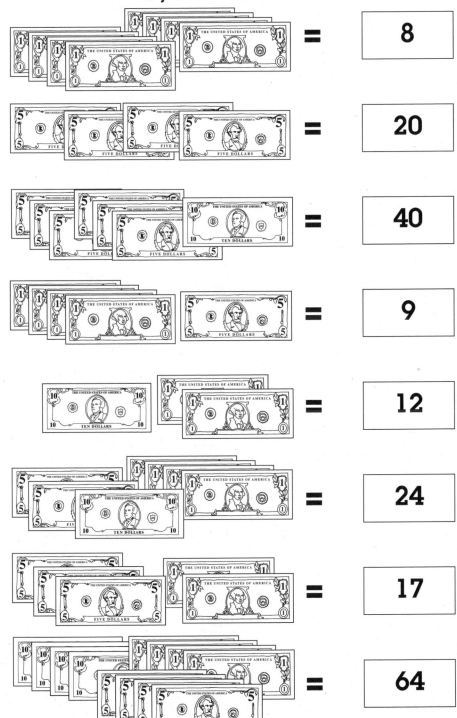

# TWENTIES, FIFTIES & 100s

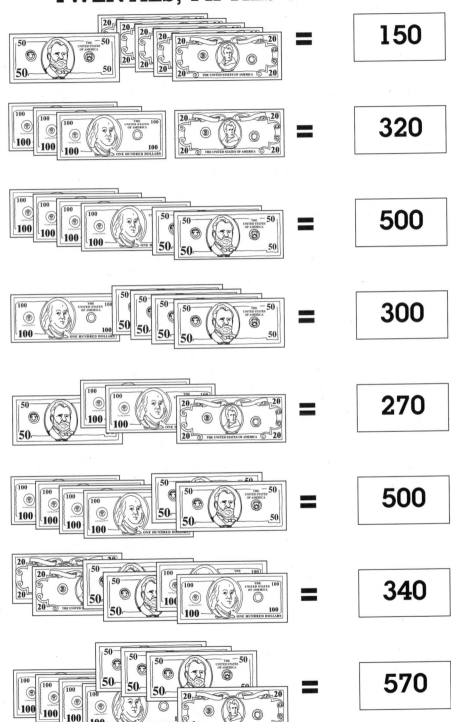

# MIXED CENTS

 = 65

 = 23

 = 47

 = 82

 = 36

 = 16

 = 77

= 94

# MIXED DOLLARS

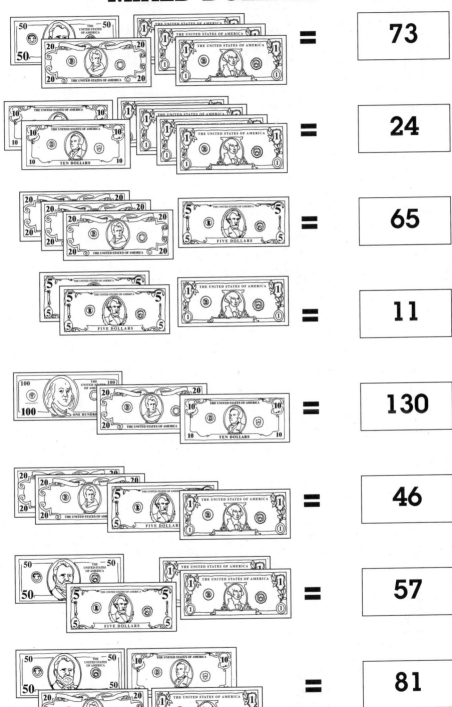

| | |
|---|---|
| = | 73 |
| = | 24 |
| = | 65 |
| = | 11 |
| = | 130 |
| = | 46 |
| = | 57 |
| = | 81 |

# MIXED DOLLARS & CENTS

 = **1.31**

 = **62.23**

 = **25.19**

 = **86.95**

 = **13.06**

 = **57.67**

 = **121.54**

 = **30.77**

# MIXED DOLLARS & CENTS

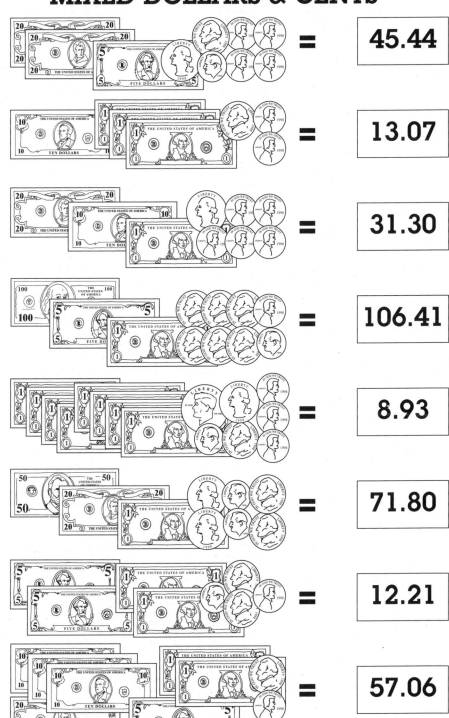

# MIXED DOLLARS & CENTS

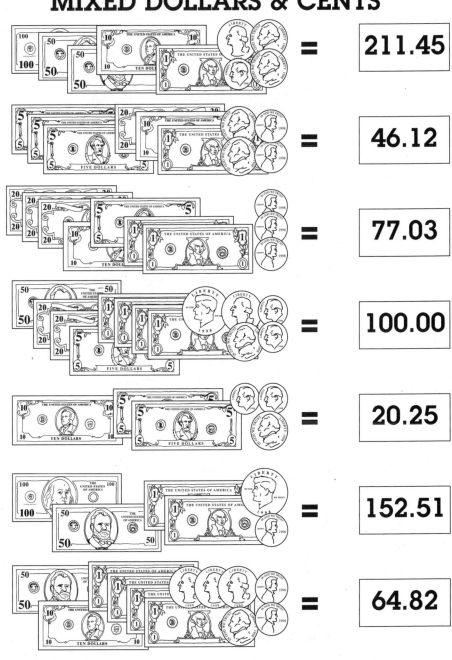